Fish-it3

Published by:
Arc Publishing and Print
166 Knowle Lane
Sheffield S11 9SJ

Produced By: Chris Keeling

Whilst every effort has been made to ensure the contents of this
publication are accurate at the time of publishing.
Arc Publishing and Print and those involved in producing the content
of "Fish-It 3 East Riding of Yorkshire" cannot be held responsible for
any errors, omissions or changes in the details of this guide or for the
consequences of any reliance on the information provided in it. We
have tried to ensure accuracy in this guide but things do change and
we would be grateful if readers could advise us of any inaccuracies
they have found.

ISBN: 978-1-906722-04-3

ACKNOWLEDGEMENTS

I would like to thank the following for there
help in producing this guide:

Bradford No1 Angling Association.
Hull & District Anglers' Association.
Doncaster & District Angling Association.
Jim Steele for venue information.

All fishery owners and angling clubs who have kindly
provided information and to those that gave permission to
use images from their websites.

Arc Publishing and Print
166 Knowle Lane
Sheffield
S11 9SJ

C O N T E N T S

ACKNOWLEDGEMENTS 2

CONTENTS 3

WELCOME...4

ABOUT THIS GUIDE 5

SPECIES / SYMBOLS 6

GETTING STARTED 7

KNOTS 10

EAST RIDING OF YORKSHIRE MAP 11

VENUES 12

FISHING TERMS 56

POLE FISHING FOR THE BEGINNER..........58

H&DAA RULES 59

CLUB MEMBERSHIP COSTS 60

FISHING TACKLE SHOPS...........................61

INDEX 62

W E L C O M E

Welcome to Fish-it 3 (East Riding of Yorkshire). This third book in the series covers some of the best fishing venues in the country-from Fishponds Fishery near Bridlington to the Aire and Calder Canal near Goole. This guide is aimed at the angler, like myself, who loves trying new fishing locations.

I wanted to produce a book that gives a good idea of what a fishing venue has to offer thus avoiding disappointment when reaching your destination.

There is plenty of information, along with photos of most venues, so hopefully you will find the ideal water to suit your method of fishing.

New fishing lakes are opening all the time and, with the well hidden and un-advertised ponds there is possibly enough for yet another guide.

If you have details of a venue and you would like it included in a future publication, please fill in the form at the back of this guide.

Hopefully you will find Fish-it 3 helpful in trying new places to fish.

Chris Keeling

I have tried to ensure the accuracy of this guide but things do change very quickly so if you know of any inaccuracies or any fisheries I have not included I would be grateful if you could fill out and return the form at the back of the guide.

A B O U T   T H I S   G U I D E

To help you locate a fishery, in the East Riding of Yorkshire area. I have placed a float symbol with its location number on the area map. See page 11

Each page contains details of a fishery,
with information on the following:

Ticket Price: Day ticket costs plus details on OAPs, disabled and junior concessions

Directions: Usually from the nearest city or town, or from the closest motorway junction.

Description: A brief outline of what the fishery looks like plus details on features such as islands, depths and the best places to fish.

Types of Fish: List of species present, many with estimated weights.

Rules/Bans: The restrictions set by the fishery on type of baits, hooks etc.

Number of Lakes: The number of waters available to fish at the venue.

Facilities: What is available at each location i.e. cafe.

Telephone: The number of the owner, angling club secretary or match organiser.

Sat Nav: Post Codes for use on satellite navigation systems.

SPECIES / SYMBOLS

Most commonly found in
the East Riding of Yorkshire area.

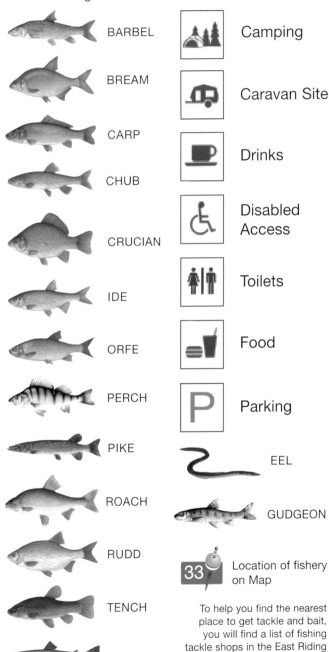

BARBEL

BREAM

CARP

CHUB

CRUCIAN

IDE

ORFE

PERCH

PIKE

ROACH

RUDD

TENCH

TROUT

Camping

Caravan Site

Drinks

Disabled
Access

Toilets

Food

Parking

EEL

GUDGEON

33 Location of fishery
on Map

To help you find the nearest
place to get tackle and bait,
you will find a list of fishing
tackle shops in the East Riding
of Yorkshire on pages 61

6

GETTING STARTED

Fishing is enjoyed by many people as both a sport and a hobby. Basically anglers can be divided into three types.
Firstly the pleasure angler who fishes just for the relaxation and fun - enjoying their surroundings but unworried about the number of fish caught (as long as they get a few).
The match angler is competitive and has a wide knowledge of the sport. He enjoys competing against other anglers and has an impressive collection of tackle which enables him to fish large lakes, small ponds, canals and rivers.
The specimen angler or hunter is a loner, usually intent on catching a large fish. Most specialise in a particular species - eg. carp, pike, barbel.
The specimen carp hunter can spend thousands on his tackle and many hours making special rigs in his bid to catch that really big fish.
Most people, however, take up fishing purely for pleasure.
To get started you will need the following:-

Rod: Most beginners start with a match rod. A good choice would be a 12' carbon fibre rod. Your local tackle shop will advise you, ask the assistant to fit a reel to the rod. It should be comfortable to hold and feel well balanced. Carbon composite rods are cheaper than the carbon rods. In the long run it pays to get a good carbon rod.

Reel: There is a wide range of reels. Again ask for advice from the tackle shop or try one of the many angling forums on the internet. You will get sound advice from more experienced anglers. Begin with a fixed spool reel which will cost you between £15 and £25. Most fixed reels come with two spools. Put 3lb line on one and a heavier line (6lb) on the other for catching larger fish.

Keepnet: Ideal if you like to see your catch when you've finished fishing. Make sure you get a large net and fully open it whilst in the water - this allows the fish room to move. Make sure it is at least 8' in length. They are made in either round or rectangular shape. Some have adjustable legs for use on sloping banks. Note, many fisheries don't allow keepnets except in matches. Check fishery rules.

Landing Net: This is a vital piece of equipment for landing a hooked fish. Again there are various sizes available. Don't buy one to small or you will have a problem landing that unexpected big carp! Never attempt to swing fish to hand, get into the habit of landing all fish no matter how small. Swinging in larger fish will damage the fish and could also break your rod.

Floats: There are many types of float to chose from, but wagglers are the most popular. The best way to attach them to your line is by fixing a float adaptor, this is a piece of silicon tubing with a swivel eye, which allows the float to be changed without breaking down the rest of your tackle. Most floats are made of plastic, balsa or peacock quill. For faster flowing waters many anglers use stick floats.

Seatbox: This is useful, not only as a seat but as a storage place for your fishing gear. The Shakespeare seatbox is very popular. It is made of light weight plastic with good storage space and two detachable trays - ideal for the beginner. More expensive boxes have hinged lids and separate storage compartments for rigs, plus adjustable legs for use on uneven ground.

Line: The line is a thin string made from a single fibre, this is called monofilament line. It comes in different colours but clear is the commonly used type. Monofilament degrades with time and can weaken when exposed to heat and sunlight. When stored on a spool for a long time, it may come off the fishing reel in coils or loops. It is advisable to change monofilament line at regular intervals to prevent degradation. Load your reel with 3 to 4lb line for float fishing. If you targeting heavier fish then use 6 to 8lb line.

Hooks: There is an enormous variety of fish hooks that will be on display at your local tackle shop. Buy hooks that are already tied to a nylon hook length and make sure you get barbless ones as they are much easier to remove from the fish. Size 22 (small) are ideal for small roach and perch, upto size 14 for larger fish.

Rodrests: These attach to a bankstick which is a pointed metal stick with a universal threaded end. There are many types of rests, just chose one that will support your rod comfortably.

Shot: Shot comes in sizes SSG to No8 and can be bought separately or in multi-size shot dispensers. The bigger shot is used to fix your waggler at the correct depth position on your line. The lighter smaller shot is used to sink your line and set the appearance of your float on the water surface.

Plummet: A plummet is a weight which is used to accurately measure the depth of water you are going to fish. They are attached to your hook. If the float disappears after you have cast in, then you are set too shallow and need to move your float up the line.

Disgorger: This is used to safely remove the hook from the mouth of a fish. The plastic barrel type are best. Simply slide the disgorger down the line until contact is made with the hook bend. Give it a slight push and out will come the hook.

Fishing Licence: Anyone over the age of 12 will need an Environment Agency Rod Licence. This allows you to fish for coarse fish but you will also require permission from the owner of the fishing rights. You can get this either by club membership or by purchasing a day ticket. Rod licences run for twelve months beginning on 31st March. Eight day and one day licences are also available. You can these from post offices or on line @ environment-agency.gov.uk/fish.
Adult licences cost £25.00 for a full year.
8 day licences are £9.00
1 day licences are £3.50
Junior (12-16 years) are only £5.00
There are also concessionary licences for people aged 65 or over.
(Check the Environment Agency web site for the latest prices)

In the cooler months you will need warm and waterproof clothing. An umbrella is also a good idea - get one that tilts. There are a few rules to keep everyone happy. Close all gates. Have respect for the landowner who has given permission for you to use his land and most importantly don't leave litter - especially discarded line and hooks.

Good fishing!

Blood Knot

This knot can be used to join two lines together, start by overlapping the ends of the two lines.

Thread the end of your line through the eye of your hook.

Twist one end round the other line four times and pass it between the two lines.

Do the same with the other end of line, making sure the previous step does not come undone.

Before pulling tight wet the knot to lubricate this also make it hold better. Trim off the two ends.

Half Blood Knot

Used mainly for joining hook to line.

Continue to loop the free end over the line about four times.

Pass the loose end between the eye of the hook and the first loop.

Pull on the loose end to tighten. Trim the line.

Double Overhand loop

This knot is used to create a loop at the end of a line. Also known as the surgeon's loop.

To begin, double the end of the line back against itself.

Tie an overhand knot in the doubled line.

The doubled end should then be tucked through the loop again.

Pull the knot as tight as possible and trim of the end.

Water Knot

This knot can also be known as the surgeon's knot. It is useful for joining a lighter hook line to your mainline

Hold the ends of the two lines alongside each other so that they overlap by about six inches.

Take hold of the two lines and make a wide loop.

Holding the two lines together. Pass the ends of the line through the loop four times.

Pull the lines tightly so that the loop makes a knot. Trim the two ends.

East Riding of Yorkshire

Aire & Calder Canal	1
Barmston Farm Fishing Lake	2
Beverley Canal	3
Blue Lagoon Pond	4
Brandesburton Ponds No 2	5
Brandesburton Ponds No 3+4	5
Brickyard Pond	6
Burshill A Pond	7
Burshill B Pond	8
Burton Constable	8
Driffield Canal	9
Emmotland Ponds	10
Fishponds Fishery	11
Fossehill Fisheries	12
Greaves End Pond	13
Halcyon House	14
Halsham Ponds	15
Hornsea Mere	16
Lakeminster Park Lakes	17
Lakeside	18
Lambwath Lakes	19
Market Weighton Canal	20
Moorfield Farm Fishery	21
Motorway Pond	22
Newbridge Lakes	23
Oakland Waters	24
Pastures Fish Pond	25
Rainbow Lake	26
Risby Park Fisheries	27
Rush Lyvars Lake	28
Sandholme Lodge	29
Southfield Reservoir	30
Star Carr Fishery	31
Straddlethorpe Pond	32
Wansford Fishery	33
Westfield Park	34
Westlands Lakes	35
West Cowick Pond	36
Wholsea Grange Fishery	37
Willitoft Fishery	38
Windmill Pond	39
Woodall's Pond	40
Rose Cottage Pond	41

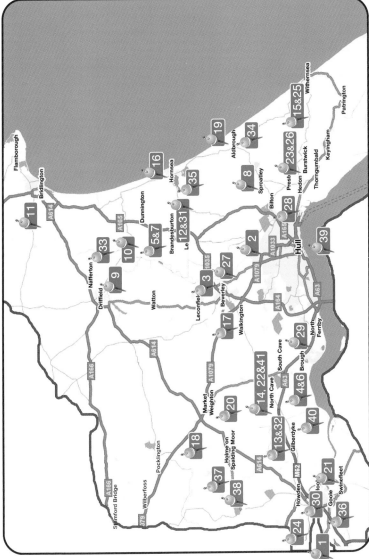

11

Aire & Calder Canal
Heck Bridge to Crow Croft Bridge.

Ticket Price: Membership prices, see on page 60

Direction: Leave the M62 at Junction 34 and follow the A19 north for 1.5 miles then turn left onto A645 Weeland Road. For Great Heck turn left into

Long Lane after two miles. Access is down track on the left just before railway. Park on the bankside after bungalow. For Pollington Road Bridge carry on over railway along Heck and Pollington Lane for approx 1.25 miles then turn left into Pinfold Lane. At the end turn left into Main Street then immediately right into Bridge Lane- canal is 400 yards further on. For Crow Croft Bridge carry on along Pollington Main Street and at the end turn right into Crow Croft Lane. After 500yds. go over canal and turn right- Crow Croft bridge is 0.5 miles further.

Description: Great Heck. North bank, access via lane next to railway, parking on bank between bungalow and rail bridge. You can fish in two directions from the carpark- down towards Pollington road bridge and up towards Great Heck Road bridge. No cars allowed under the rail bridge and no fishing under or near powerlines. South Bank. There is limited access and no cars on the bank. Pollington Road Bridge. There is limited parking on the north bank - fishing is allowed upstream towards Heck. There is no fishing on the north bank downstream and no fishing at all on the south bank. Crowcroft Bridge. South bank upstream, access under the road bridge, fishing up to the lock. Parking is on road side which runs parallel to canal downstream of the road bridge. North bank upstream, limited access via car park, of about six pegs. No fishing in boat moorings.

Telephone: 01274 421786

Facilities: Sat Nav: DN14 0BA

Information kindly supplied by Bradford No1 Angling Association.

Barmston Farm Fishing Lake
Barmston Lane, Woodmansey, Beverley.

Ticket Price: £5.00 per day. £3.00 after 5pm.
Under 16 £3.00 and £1.50 after 5pm.

Directions: Located in Woodmansey on the A1174 (Hull Road) from Beverley to Hull. Turn down Barmston Lane on the corner next to the church and follow the road round.(See map).

Description: Set within a privately owned static caravan site, this two acre lake has been extensively stocked with a good mix of fish. Many anglers come here to try and catch the carp which reach the 30lb mark. Most species in this lake are huge with bream and tench both around 10-11lb in weight. Perch reach 3lb and the roach and rudd to nearly 2lb. Feeder fishing is well worth trying for the carp using a hair rig with meat or corn. Float fish for the tench and bream with bread or red maggot - this works best on a warm day. There are caravans and cottages to rent if you wanted a longer stay.

Types of Fish: Tench to 10lb, bream to 11lb. Good sized roach rudd. Carp to 30lb with perch and ide making up the remaining species.

Rules/Bans: Barbless hooks and no keepnets.

Facilities: [P] [♿] [🚐] [🚻]   [2]

Number of Lakes: One   **Sat Nav:** HU17 0TP

Telephone: 01482 863566

Beverley Canal

Waterside Road, Beverley.

Ticket Price: Day tickets £3.00. Concessions £1.00. on the bank.

Directions: From Beverley, and take the A1174 south, heading towards Kingston. Go across the Canal Bridge and turn left at the Total petrol station. This will take you into Waterside Road. Carry on down the track and park somewhere on the verge.

Description: This venue consists of a productive one mile of canal which has lily pads, reeds and trees. The average depth is about eight feet, and it's about 120 feet wide. There are lock gates so expect some flow when they are open. For bream or tench fish to the lily pads with caster, corn or bread. Put in bait little and often. Perch, roach and eels go well on maggot. Fish under the boats for the chub.

Types of Fish: Few carp to 14lb, pike to 25lb, bream to 7lb, chub to 5lb, tench to 6lb, perch and crucian to 3lb, eels to 4lb, roach to 2lb 6oz, and rudd.

Rules/Bans: Barbless hooks only. No keepnets.

Facilities: P ♿ **Number of Lakes:** One mile

Telephone: 07976 779983   **Sat Nav:** HU17 0PP

Blue Lagoon Pond
Broomfleet.

Ticket Price: Membership permits and prices on page 60

Directions: Situated at Broomfleet landing, Broomfleet.
See map below for Hull and District Anglers' Association waters.

Description: This fishery is situated at Broomfleet Landing and is a popular water of about 2 acres and offers an alternative to the nearby Market Weighton Canal fishery. This old clay pit has a depth of around 8 to 12ft., with bottom weed sometimes causing problems during the summer. The main interest is bream with occasional large catches being made, particularly early in the season. Roach, perch and eels are also present with some small pike. Most of the pegs provide comfortable fishing, and there are two adjacent to the car park which are suitable for disabled anglers.

Types of Fish: Bream, roach, perch, pike and eels.

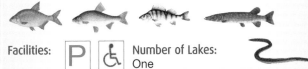

Facilities: ☐ P ☐ ♿   **Number of Lakes:** One

Rules/Bans: Full list of rules can be found on page 59

Telephone: 07976 779983

Information kindly supplied by Hull and District Anglers' Association.

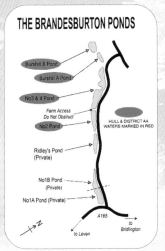

THE BRANDESBURTON PONDS

Burshill B Pond
Burshill A Pond
No3 & 4 Pond
Farm Access
Do Not Obstruct
No2 Pond
HULL & DISTRICT AA
WATERS MARKED IN RED
Ridley's Pond
(Private)
No1B Pond
(Private)
No1A Pond (Private)
A165
to Leven
to Bridlington

THE NEWPORT, NORTH CAVE & BROOMFLEET FISHERIES

Motorway Pond
M62
to Hull
B1230
Thornton Lane
Weighton Lane
Newport village
Market Weighton Canal
Private Pond No Fishing
No Access
Blue Lagoon
Brickyard Pond
Tilery Lake

Brandesburton Ponds

No 2 Pond.   Hempholme Lane, Brandesburton.

Ticket Price: Membership permits and prices on page 60

Directions: Follow the A165 (Hull to Bridlington) road. On entering the village of Brandesburton, take the first left turn down Hempholme Lane. Follow this road for less than 1 mile. No 2 Pond is on the left hand side.

Description: No 2 Pond is a mature gravel pit of about two acres holding a good head of sizeable roach and perch. The roach fishing tends to be at its best early in the year when pole-fished maggots can produce some excellent sport. The water has seen the capture of some large perch in recent years, with fish up to 3lb 10oz reported - you can't go far wrong with a good lobworm here. There are also pike and eels present and a number of large carp.

Types of Fish: Roach, perch, pike, eels, and carp

Rules/Bans: Full list of rules can be found on page 59

Facilities: P ♿   **Number of Lakes:** One

Telephone: 07976 779983

5

See map on page 15 for Hull and District Anglers' Association waters.

Information kindly supplied by Hull and District Anglers' Association.

Brandesburton Ponds

No 3 & 4 Pond. Hempholme Lane, Brandesburton.

Ticket Price: Membership permits and prices on page 60

Directions: Follow the A165 (Hull to Bridlington) road. On entering the village of Brandesburton take the first left turn down Hempholme Lane. Follow this road for less than 1 mile. Nos. 3 & 4 Pond are on the left hand side.

Description: Nos. 3 & 4 Pond are about eight acres and this picturesque water is one of the Association's most popular fisheries. The water holds a large head of carp which have grown well since their introduction a few years ago. They mainly consist of upper doubles but there are also several 20lb-plus fish. This is an ideal water for both beginner and the more advanced angler. The carp will respond to most baits and, given the right conditions, several fish can be taken in a session. Throughout the winter the water is popular with pike anglers who can expect to catch some good-sized fish. Large numbers of bream are also present, with bags of over 100lb having being reported. Fish up to 9lb have been taken and, generally, they are not fussy and will readily take maggots, casters, sweetcorn, worm and even boilies. For the best results fish sweetcorn or casters over a bed of groundbait and wait for the fish to move in.

Types of Fish: Roach, tench, bream, perch, pike, eels, carp.

Rules/Bans: Full list of rules can be found on page 59

Facilities: 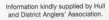 **Telephone:** 07976 779983

Information kindly supplied by Hull and District Anglers' Association.

See map on page 15 for Hull and District Anglers' Association waters.

17

Brickyard Pond
Broomfleet.

Ticket Price: Membership permits and prices on page 60

Directions: Situated at Broomfleet, close to the Market Weighton Canal. Access via Broomfleet village, past Blue Lagoon Pond and along the road adjacent to the Canal. Cross over the bridge and turn immediately left. Drive for a short distance along the track with the Canal on the left and the pond with submerged trees on your right. (See map on page ?? for Hull and District Anglers' Association waters).

Description: Brickyard Pond holds some excellent fish stocks. It is a very old and mature clay pit surrounded by trees. Consequently there is a thick bed of silt over much of the bottom. The pond is split down the middle by a band of reeds, but fish can migrate between the two areas.
Depths fall off quickly from the margins and are generally between 10 and 15ft. There are two sunken roads, about 10ft wide, created during the excavation of the clay, which have little or no silt on them. They are around 7ft below the surface.

Types of Fish: There are tench over 6lb, bream over 11lb, roach and rudd over 1 3/4lb, carp over 40lb and pike over 29lb. In addition there are numerous small perch and eels.

Rules/Bans: Full list of rules can be found on page 59

Facilities: P ♿   **Number of Lakes:** One

Telephone: 07976 779983

See map on page 15 for Hull and District Anglers' Association waters.

Information kindly supplied by Hull and District Anglers' Association.

Burshill A Pond
Hempholme Lane, Brandesburton.

Ticket Price: Membership permits and prices on page 60

Directions: Follow the A165 (Hull to Bridlington) road. On entering the village of Brandesburton, take the first left turn down Hempholme Lane. Follow this road for less than 1 mile. Burshill A Pond is on the left hand side.

Description: Burshill A is a pond about 1.5 acres and has been created and developed as a pleasure fishery. Unlike the neighbouring pits it is shallow and flat-bottomed, and has been heavily stocked with small fish with the intention of making the fishing easy. All the swims are easily accessible and have timber staging. The pond is also well sheltered from the wind. If you like to fish in comfort and have a constant bend in your rod, this is the place for you.

Types of Fish: Heavily stocked with small fish.

Rules/Bans: Full list of rules can be found on page 59

Facilities: **Number of Lakes:** One

Telephone: 07976 779983

See map on page 15 for Hull and District Anglers' Association waters.

Information kindly supplied by Hull and District Anglers' Association.

Burshill B Pond
Hempholme Lane, Brandesburton.

Ticket Price: Membership permits and prices on page 60

Directions: Follow the A165 (Hull to Bridlington) road. On entering the village of Brandesburton, take the first left turn down Hempholme Lane. Follow this road for less than 1 mile. Burshill B Pond is on the left hand side.

Description: Burshill B is one of two ponds in the Burshill Fishery part of the Brandesburton Complex. A mature fairly shallow pond of about 2.5 acres. It is primarily a tench water but does contain roach, rudd, pike and the odd carp. It becomes very weedy in summer. Early morning or evening are the best times for tench fishing and, although they tend not to be caught in large numbers, those that are caught are often of a good size. 5lb fish are not uncommon and last season a fish of 8lb 2oz was reported. This is another fishery which received a major facelift in 1999, with several new swims being built and the paths cleared. Well worth a look if tench is your quarry.

Facilities: P ♿ **Number of Lakes:** One

Rules/Bans: Full list of rules can be found on page 59

Telephone: 07976 779983

See map on page 15 for Hull and District Anglers' Association waters.

Information kindly supplied by Hull and District Anglers' Association.

Burton Constable
Holiday Park, Sproatley.

Ticket Price: Day Tickets - 1 Rod £6.00 - 2 Rods £7.00 Junior / OAP £3.00. Weekly £18.00. Season £65.00 Season OAP £60.00

Directions: From the Humber Bridge follow the A63 through Hull towards Withernsea. Turn left at the start of the A1033 going towards Preston. Turn left at the lights in Preston, then pick up the signs to Burton Constable. In Sproatley turn left down Park Road.

Description: The lake provides excellent sport with a multitude of fish to catch such as Pike, Tench, Carp, Bream, Roach and Perch with a continuous programme of restocking. Fishing permits are available from the Reception.

Types of Fish: Bream, perch, roach, tench, rudd and carp.

Rules/Bans: Barbless hooks only. No keepnets. No fishing from the bridge. No night fishing. Ask for further pike fishing rules.

Facilities:

Number of Lakes: One   **Telephone:** 01964 562508

8

Sat Nav: HU11 4LN

Driffield Canal
Wansford near Driffield.

Ticket Price: Membership permits and prices on page 60

Directions: Access to most of the Canal is easy as it runs alongside the B1249 Driffield to North Frodingham road. There is good parking in Wansford village where there are purpose build fishing stances for anglers with disabilities. Parking elsewhere can be more difficult, although parking on the grass verge is possible in places.

Description: This pretty waterway is about four miles in length with the main fishing area centred around the village of Wansford. The canal holds good stocks of roach, perch, bream and trout - there is also the odd carp, pike and grayling present. In places the canal is badly silted and when water levels are low it can be reduced to a mere trickle.   For most of the year, the water is very clear which makes locating fish easy, but in the summer this allows profuse weed growth.

Types of Fish: Roach, perch, bream, trout, pike and some carp.

Facilities: P & 9

Rules/Bans: Full list of rules can be found on page 59

Telephone: 07976 779983

Information kindly supplied by Hull and District Anglers' Association.

Emmotland Ponds

Emmotland, North Frodingham, Driffield.

Ticket Price: Day ticket for Pond 4 - £5.00

Directions: From Beverley head north on the A1035. At White Cross the road changes to the A135. Go through Brandesburton. After two miles turn left onto Grange Road. Take your next left into Cross Road. Turn Left at Emmotland. Look for the fishery on your right hand side.

Description: Three of the four ponds here are for the serious carp and predator angler, for which you are advised to book before setting off. Pond 4 is a well stocked two acre water, which has 30 pegs and can be fished on a day ticket. Night fishing is available on Ponds 1, 2 and 3.

Types of Fish: Large specimen carp to over 45lbs. Bream, Ide, Perch, Roach, Tench, Crucian, and pike.

Rules/Bans: Barbless or crushed barbs. No lead core No keepnets. Large unhooking / Carp mats compulsory. No braid on main line. No sacking. No nuts. No fixed rigs. No litterbugs.

Number of Lakes: Four   **Sat Nav:** YO25 8JS

Telephone: 01262 488226

Facilities: Tackle shop on site

Fishponds Fishery
Woldgate, Bridlington.

Ticket Price: Day tickets £5.00. £2 per extra rod. Concessions £4.00.

Directions: From Driffield head towards Bridlington. When you see a sign for Bridlington Town Centre, turn left which is signposted Woldgate. This is little more than a single track road and the water is about 3/4 of mile on the right. Take your time as it is easy to miss.

Description: There are three ponds to fish, with the added attraction of having some trees for shelter from the sea breeze. They all have a shallow depth which makes them idea for summer sport and are heavily stocked with mirror, common and crucian carp. If you want to stay longer there are caravans on site.

Types of Fish: Main species are carp, bream, tench and plenty of silver fish.

Rules/Bans: No person under 18 unless accompanied. No keepnets, and barbless hooks only.

Facilities:  **Number of Lakes:** Three

Telephone: 01262 605873   **Sat Nav:** YO16 4XE
to the nearest farm.

11

Fossehill Fisheries
Catwick Lane, Brandesburton.

Ticket Price: Adult day ticket £6.00   Junior / OAP / Disabled day ticket £4.50

Directions: From Beverley, head east on the A1035. At White Cross the road becomes the A165. When you reach the roundabout in Brandesburton, take the last exit (right). This is Catwick Lane.

Description: Set within Watersedge Park, this award winning fishery has plenty to offer for both pleasure and match angler. It has five ponds which range between 1/2 and 3 acres. Depths vary from 3 feet to 16 feet. All are well stocked with a good variety of coarse fish.

Types of Fish: Carp 34lb+, Bream 10lb+, Rudd 2lb+, Chub 5lb+, Barbel 5lb+, Roach 2lb+, Tench 8lb+, Pike 25lb+ Perch 2lb+, Eels 5lb+, Ide 3lb+.

Number of Lakes: Five

Rules/Bans: Two rods maximum. No keep-nets. No boilies. No ground bait. No barbed hooks. No litter. No fires. Children must be accompanied by an adults. Fishing from designated pegs only.

Facilities:

Telephone: 01964 544357   **Sat Nav:** YO25 8RY

12

Greaves End Pond
Eastrington.

Ticket Price: Day Tickets £7.00. Concessions £4.00.

Directions: From Goole take the A614 heading towards Market Weighton. When you reach Howden turn onto the B1230 signposted Beverley. Turn left to Eastrington, at the post office turn left again onto Carr lane. Turn right at the crossroads and follow the road to the fishery.

Description: This 2.5 acre pond has a depth of around 9 feet but I would fish the top corner near the carpark, where it is nearer 4 feet. Various species are present including some large carp to 30lb. Try fishing close to the few small islands, with large chunks of meat if you want the carp. This is a lovely lake set in nice surroundings, well worth a try.

Types of Fish: Large carp, bream to 8lb and Tench to 6lb . Roach and rudd run to 2lb, with perch, crucian and ide making up the remainder of the stock. The water holds catfish that run to 25lb.

Rules/Bans: No loosefed boilies, no keepnets, barbless hooks.

Number of Lakes: One

Facilities:

13

Telephone: 01430 410619   **Sat Nav:** DN14 7QW

Halcyon House
Newport.

Ticket Price: Day Ticket £5.00. No concessions.

Directions: Come off the M62 at junction 38. Take the B1230 to Newport. Turn Right after the 30 MPH Speed limit ends onto Thimble Hall Lane, at T-Junction turn Right. The pond is located 300 yards on the left.

Description: This two and a half acre pond is stuffed with fish and some heavy ones are amongst them. There are roach, rudd, tench, carp and perch. plus a large head of bream. This pond seems to be set up with families in mind and younger anglers are welcomed. It is ideal for the beginners as in the warmer months you can catch at every chuck. Bread or maggots must be taken for the roach and perch. Sweetcorn and worm for the tench. There is a toilet and other facilities available for the more seasoned angler.

Types of Fish: Roach, perch, tench, rudd and bream.

Facilities: P ♿ 🚹

Rules/Bans: Barbless Hooks only. No Keepnets. No litter or fires. Fishing from sun up to sun down. Night fishing by arrangement only.

Telephone: 01430 441765   **Sat Nav:** HU15 2RN

Halsham Ponds
Dalton Lane, Halsham.

Ticket Price: Day Ticket £4.00. No concessions.
Night fishing £8.00 (advanced bookings only)

Directions: Take A1033 east out of Hull. At Hedon take the B1362. When you reach Halsham turn right onto Dalton Lane. You will find the ponds behind the Halsham Arms.

Description: Three ponds in this lovely small village, set behind the local pub - perfect for a pint if the weather turns. The ponds are named Island Pond, Old Pond and Carpark Pond. Carpark Pond is the deepest at 15ft. in the middle. All produce a good bag of fish, but its advisable to get there early as these are fairly small ponds and it can get busy. Fishing with double maggot close to the reeds seemed to be working for most anglers.

Types of Fish: Carp to 27lb, tench to 4lb+, bream, rudd and roach. The owner is currently adding more stock which includes barbel, ide and chub.

Facilities:

Rules/Bans: Barbless Hooks only. No groundbait.
No Keepnets.

Telephone: 01964 670481   **Sat Nav:** HU12 0DG

Hornsea Mere

Hornsea.

Ticket Price: Day tickets £5.00 per person. Boat hire £7.00 plus £5.00 per person.

Direction: Coming into Hornsea on the B1244, you will see the Mere on your right hand side. It is well signposted.

Description: This natural lake is 250 acres and is the largest in Yorkshire. There is a stretch of bank, about 400 yards which is the easiest area to fish. Note there is no fishing from the jetties. The best way is to hire a rowing boat if the water is not too rough. Plenty of roach to around 2lbs can be caught on bread or of course maggot. You could get lucky and hook a carp which reach 25lbs but locating them is very difficult. Many anglers come for the pike, with good numbers around 10lb and the odd few reaching 30lbs.

Types of Fish: Pike, carp, bream, roach and perch.

Rules/Bans: No fishing before 9.00 am or after 5.00pm. No livebaiting.

Facilities: **Number of Lakes:** One

Telephone: 01964 533277   **Sat Nav:** HU18 1AX   16

Lakeminster Park Lakes
Hull Road, Beverley.

Ticket Price: Day Tickets £4.00 must be purchased from reception on site before fishing.

Directions: Signposted from Beverley. If you take the A1174 road towards Hull, you can't miss it.

Description: Simple tactics work well on both of the two lakes here at Lakeminster. If you forget maggots, make sure you have some bread as both will catch plenty of fish. Its an ideal place for the beginner as both lakes are stuffed with a variety of species. The waters are situated on a holiday park, so the facilities you will find there are very good. A few anglers were fishing close in, using sweetcorn and seemed to be catching tench, which I was told reached the 6lb mark. There is a new housing development planned near here, so please check beforehand that fishing is available.

Types of Fish: Roach to 2lb, chub to 2lb, carp to 25lb, crucian to 2lb, tench to 6lb, bream and perch to 3lb.

Rules/Bans: Barbless hooks. No carp in keepnets.

Facilities:

Number of Lakes: Two

Telephone: 01482 882655   **Sat Nav:** HU17 0PN

Lakeside
Lakeside Caravan Park & Coarse Fishery, Bielby.

Ticket Price: £7.00 non residents. £6.00 for residents. Max of two rods.

Directions: Lakeside is signposted from the A1079 York to Hull Rd. 12 miles from York.

Description: The fishery is six acres in size. It is an old gravel pit and as such has a wealth of underwater contours for both the fish and the angler to explore. As you can see from the photograph, the well spaced out pegs have plenty of margin features to target plus a small island to fish upto. Many of these flagged pegs are suitable for disabled anglers.

Types of Fish: It contains carp to 30lb+, tench 10lb+ bream 12lb+. As well as ide, crucian carp, roach, rudd, chub, and perch.

Rules/Bans: No anglers under 16 years old. Barbless hooks only. Groundbait in moderation. No Boilies. Do not throw cigarette ends either into the water or on the bank. No radios, dogs, fires, wading or swimming. No litter. Open 7am to 9pm or dusk, which ever comes first.

Facilities:

Sat Nav: YO42 4JP

Number of Lakes: One   **Telephone:** 01759 318100

18

www.lakesidewebsite.com

Lambwath Lakes
Aldbrough.

Ticket Price: Day tickets £5.50 Adult. £3.50 Concessions

Directions: Head out of Hull on the A165 going north. Turn right onto the B1238 to Aldbrough. When you reach Aldbrough turn right again into Seaside Road. Follow this road and just before the caravan site, turn right to the fishery.

Description: A great set of ponds to try, but wrap up warm, there's not much cover from the north sea winds. Caravan Pond is the largest with 40 pegs and also the deepest at around 12 feet. Most species can be caught with some good tench over 4lb. Moat Pond is my favourite, which has a depth of 5 feet and holds many good sized carp to 16lb. There are also plenty of rudd to 1lb. All of these ponds provide excellent sport.

Types of Fish: All the waters have a similar stocking policy with carp (most varieties), roach, perch, bream, rudd, ide and some good tench.

Rules/Bans: No keepnets, boilies, flavourings or colouring, natural coloured maggots only. Landing nets to be dipped prior to fishing. Barbless hooks only. No night fishing.

Facilities: **Number of Lakes:** Five

Telephone: 01964 527740   **Sat Nav:** HU11 4SA   19

Market Weighton Canal
Between Weighton Lock and Sodhouse Lock.

Ticket Price: Day tickets must be obtained in advance and are available from Newport News, the newsagents on Main Road, Newport. The shop has extensive open hours including Sunday mornings. (Permit prices see page 60)

Directions: Between Weighton Lock, where it discharges into the Humber and the Sodhouse Lock. Parking is available in a number of areas, including Broomfleet Landing, Landing Lane, Canalside West and Canalside East in Newport.

Description: A nine mile section of the canal offers excellent fishing along most of this length. The most popular sections tend to be near to the main access points. However consistent fishing can be had by those prepared to travel away from the most regularly fished areas. Angling is permitted from the east back only, except for the stretch in Newport, upstream of the A63 road bridge where angling is permitted on the west bank for the first 300 metres.
Apart from good stocks of fish, individual specimens reach respectable weights. Bream have been landed over 8lb, perch well over 3lb, roach to around 2lb, tench to 6lb and pike have been reported just short of 30lb. Occasional big carp also turn up with catches over 20lb.

Rules/Bans: Full list of rules can be found on page 59

Facilities: **Telephone:** 07976 779983

Information kindly supplied by Hull and District Anglers' Association.

33

Moorfield Farm Fishery

Cottingham Street, Goole.

Ticket Price: Adult day tickets £6.00 Concessions £4.00

Directions: Come off M62 at junction 36 and take the A161 south. Go over the River Don and into Old Goole. Once in Old Goole you need to turn right after the canal into Cottingham Street. Go to the end of this road and after half a mile you will reach the farm.

Description: This is what they call a prolific fishery, and they are right! The two match lakes and one pleasure lake are packed with fish, mainly carp. Renowned for fishing well all day and producing large bag weights this fishery is one not to miss. Sweetcorn and paste seem to be the favoured baits. Fish close in next to the reeds.

Types of Fish: Carp, barbel, ide, bream, roach, crucian and tench.

Rules/Bans: Barbless hooks only, no groundbait or boilies. No night fishing, no keepnets other than in matches.

Number of Lakes: Three   **Sat Nav:** DN14 8BQ

Telephone: 07710 817150

Facilities:

Motorway Pond
Thimblehall Lane, Newport.

Ticket Price: Membership permits and prices on page 60

Directions: Close to the M62 Motorway. Access through Newport village, via Thimblehall Lane or Canalside West.

Description: This fishery holds several different species and has a deserved reputation for big fish. It produced the Yorkshire carp record fish of 42lbs. 8oz. in 1999. There are also fine tench with fish over 9lb. and bream over 12lb. having been reported in the past. The water has produced a number of pike over 30lbs as well as the occasional large chub, rudd and even crucian carp. Although generally fished by specialist anglers in search of bigger fish, recent events have seen many more pleasure anglers searching out the increasing stocks of bream and tench. Large bags of quality roach to over 60lbs, with fish to almost 2lbs, are not unknown although the location is the key to success in this interesting water with many different underwater features.

Types of Fish: Carp, crucian carp, bream, pike, roach, rudd and perch

Facilities: P ♿ **Number of Lakes:** One

Rules/Bans: Night fishing is only allowed with special permits. Carp sacks and keep nets are banned from this fishery.

Telephone: 07976 779983 **Sat Nav:** HU15 2PJ

See map on page 15 for Hull and District Anglers' Association waters.

Information kindly supplied by Hull and District Anglers' Association.

Newbridge Lakes
Newbridge Rd, Burstwick.

Ticket Price: Day Fishing £5.00 (plus £1.00 per extra rod). Secure night fishing available by prior booking. £15.00 for 24 hrs.

Directions: Take A1033 east out of Hull, go through Thorngumbald. Turn left down Station Road to Burstwick, then turn right at the end of Station Road. At the mini roundabout turn left onto Newbridge Road and continue to the end of the road. Car parking is available on the complex

Description: There are three lakes here - Newbridge Lake, Hariff lake and Skeckling Lake but the specimen angler come to fish Newbridge Lake which is one of the premier carp lakes in the North of England. Nearly 7 acres in size and surrounded by 8 acres of woodland it contains, mirror carp 28lb+, common carp 30lb+, grass carp 19lb+, ghost carp 24lb+, and crucian carp to 3lb. Other species include, bream up to 14lb, roach to 3lb, rudd to 2.5lb, perch to 3.5lb, tench to 8lb, eels to 7lb, and some recently introduced chub.

Facilities: P ♿ 🚻 Bait available on site

Rules/Bans: Barbless Hooks only. No rod to be left unattended at any time. No Carp or fish over 4lb to be kept in keepnets and no fish to be held for more than 5 hours. No Nuts. No Radios. Children under 14 must be accompanied by an adult.

Telephone: 07817 058054   **Sat Nav:** HU12 9HS

Oakland Waters
Gowdall Rd, Gowdall.

Ticket Price: Coarse Fishing £6.00. Under 14s £4.00
Specimen £7.50 day - £15 per 24hrs.

Directions: From Doncaster head north on the M18. At the
intersection with the M62, head west for one junction. After
leaving the motorway head for Snaith. After the railway
station turn left into Gowdall Lane. Turn right after about a
mile onto Main Street. At Gowdall turn right onto Gowdall
Road. The lakes are about a mile along the road.

Description: With four lakes to chose from there is something
for every one. The Specimen Lake is definitely worth a try,
but make sure you book prior to setting off. My choice
would be Horseshoe Lake. As the name implies this is a
horseshoe shaped lake with an island running down the
centre. It has 39 pegs and varies in depth from 6ft-10ft with
many features to fish up to. The lake contains a mixed bag
of fishing including carp, tench, barbel, roach, rudd, bream,
ide, perch, crucian and chub.

Rules/Bans: Children under 16 must be accompanied by an
adult. Landing nets must be used. Fishing is from dawn till
dusk only unless night fishing the specimen lake.
Barbless hook only. No keepnets, unless in pre-booked
matches. Please treat the fish with the upmost care to
protect them and your fishing.

Facilities: ♿ 🚻 🅿 🍴   **Sat Nav:** DN14 0AP

Tackle shop on site

Number of Lakes: Four   **Telephone:** 01405 860756

24

Pastures Fish Pond
Halsham.

Ticket Price: Day tickets £5.00. Concessions £4.00.
Extra rod £2.00

Direction: Take the B1362 to Hedon, heading east. Keep on
the B1362, going through Burstwick. About one mile past
the signpost for Halsham, turn left into the carpark for the
fishery.

Description: There are 50 comfortable pegs to choose from at
this privately owned two and a half acre venue. There is a
central island to target with an average depth of six feet. Pole
and waggler are the best methods on this pond with
maggots, sweetcorn and meat as top hook baits.

Types of Fish: The pond holds a good head of carp, tench
and rudd along with a few perch to 2lbs. Other species
present are roach, ide, crucian to 1lb, and the odd bream.

Rules/Bans: Barbless hooks only (No Microbarbs). No
keepnet. No boilies, blood worm or joker. No groundbait.
No litter. No cat/dog meat to be used in the pond. No large
carp pellets. No surface fishing (ducks will eat the bait).

Facilities: **Number of Lakes:** One

Telephone: 01964 670489   **Sat Nav:** HU12 0DD
before 8pm

Rainbow Lake
Newbridge Rd, Burstwick.

www.rainbowlake.co.uk

Ticket Price: 1 rod £5, 2 rods £6, 3 rods £7.
24hr tickets, 2 rods £12, 3 rods £14, 4 rods £16
Juniors, Senior Citizens and Blue Badge get a £1 reduction
per rod

Directions: From Hull, head east on the A1033. Turn left onto
the B1362 a mile or so after Saltend. Stay on this road
through Hedon. Turn left into Main Street and drive through
Burstwick. Turn left into Newbridge Road and follow to the
end where you will find the lake.

Description: The best carp bait have been good quality
boillies and sweetcorn. In the warmer months try fishing off
the top with mixers as a lot have been caught using this
method. For the course fishing, maggot is the preferred
bait. Pegs 20 to 31 seem to be the most productive. Loose
feeding maggot little and often. Start fishing on the bottom
2 rod lengths out, gradually shallow up to find the fish.

Types of Fish: Large carp around 20lbs. Plenty of silver fish,
plus the bonus of bream to over 6lb.

Rules/Bans: Baiting with nuts and the use of is strictly
forbidden. Keepnets/landing nets must be dipped before
fishing. Carp over 5lb/2.3k not to be retained in keepnets.
Fishing only permitted from allocated swims.
No litter. Use bins provided. Under 14's must be
accompanied by an adult. Do not leave rods unattended.
Barbless hooks only. The Management have the right to
withdraw tickets and expel miss-users from the water.

Number of Lakes: One   **Sat Nav:** Not available.   26

Telephone: 07867 918976   **Facilities:**

Risby Park Fisheries
Dunflat Rd, Beverley.

www.risby-park.co.uk

Ticket Price: Adult day ticket £6.00. Concession/Junior £4.00

Directions: Leave the M62 at junction signposted North Cave, head through village taking signs for Beverley. At Walkington, turn right at the traffic lights located at the end of the village. The first sign for Risby is at the next right turn.

Description: The carp pond (Gillen Springs) is one of four ponds at Risby Park and is heavily stocked with mirror, common and ghost carp from 4oz. to 22lb., tench from a few ounces to 3lb., bream to 7lb. and there are also small roach and varying size ide and perch. The depth of water ranges from 5ft. around the island to 7 ft 6" at peg 1/38 end. The tench pond (The Gorse) is again heavily stocked with predominantly tench to 10 lb., ide to 3lb., skimmers to 8oz. and there are also stocks of chub and roach. This pond is particularly suitable for the younger angler as there are plenty of 'bites' to keep them interested.

Rules/Bans: Barbless hooks only, no Microbarbs or Pinched Barbs. No Rods to be left unattended at any time. Fish may be retained in keepnets for a maximum of 5 hours. No Bait restrictions (Please be sensible). After fishing do not throw excess Bait into the Pond. No Radios. One rod & one line; extra rods £2.00 on all ponds. Children under 12 must be accompanied by an adult. Fishing dawn till dusk, night fishing strictly by telephone appointment only.

Facilities: Sat Nav: HU17 8SS

Tackle shop on site

Number of Lakes: Four   **Telephone:** 07860 255981

27

Rush Lyvars Lake
Preston Rd, Hedon, Hull. HU12 8JU.

Ticket Price: £5.00 per rod. £3.00 for 2nd rod. £2.00 for 3rd rod. Pensioners £3.00. Available on the bank.

Directions: Take the A1033 from Hull and head towards Hedon. As you enter Hedon take the A1240 signposted Preston. Keep your eyes open for the fishery on your right hand side.

Description: This is a lovely fishery set on the outskirts of the village of Hedon. Try the second lake furthest from the carpark as it seems more sheltered and has more features to target. I like fishing for the tench which are a good size, but seem to hook more bream than anything else. Most types of carp are present with many species of silver fish that provide all year round sport. There are around 150 pegs , many of which are suitable for the disabled.

Types of Fish: Tench, carp, roach, rudd, perch and bream

Rules/Bans: Barbless hooks, keepnets. Night fishing by permission. No ground bait. Carp to be returned A.S.A.P

Facilities:

Number of Lakes: Two

Telephone: Mobile 0753 0951103   **Sat Nav:** HU12 8JU

Sandholme Lodge
Sandholme Lodge Holiday Park, Brough.

Ticket Price: Adult day ticket £4.00. Junior £2.50

Directions: Sandholme is situated just off Junction 38 of the M62.

Description: Two well-stocked fishing ponds with about 20 pegs, which are accessible by car and ideal for disabled visitors. Both ponds have plenty of reeds to target the various species present. These are small ponds, the biggest is only an acre in size. You can also try a 1/4 mile stretch of the River Foulness

Types of Fish: Bream, perch, roach, tench, rudd and carp.

Rules/Bans: Barbless hooks only. No keepnets.

Facilities: 🚻 ♿ 🅿️   Sat Nav: HU15 2QQ

Number of Lakes: Two   **Telephone:** 01430 440487   29

Southfield Reservoir
East Cowick.

Ticket Price: Books are valid from April 1st at £17.00 Concessionary rates £10.00 available for OAP's and Juniors.

Directions:

Description: These Reservoirs are only separated by a strip of land about 8 feet wide, but both are joined to the nearby Aire & Calder Canal. Although massive, they are only shallow - around 3 to 4 feet.

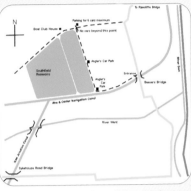

The lakes are also used by the local sailing club which means they can become a little busy at weekends, especially in summer. The good news is that they are stuffed with Bream. Bags over 50lb are not uncommon. Roach, Perch and Pike also show too.

The banks are rocky, so a platform is a good idea.

Methods: An out and out bream attack is the best ploy. Follow the wind, the Bream will move towards the shore sheltering by the more coloured water, looking for food disturbed by the wind. Traditional Brown Crumb / Brasem groundbaits work, but recently some anglers have been successful with fishmeal based groundbaits.

Squatts, Casters, Pellet, Maggot and Worm will also work. Try to fish at distance - if you can manage 60 yards it can be an advantage over those that can only fish at 40 yards. Start by putting in about 6 large feeder's worth of groundbait. Fish a smaller open ended feeder over the top and wait! Sometimes the fish just wont arrive, but usually they will. If you can manage not to loose the shoal they should remain feeding with confidence.

Roach can sometimes be caught at 10 metres plus using light rigs and loosefed caster or pinkie.

Rigs: For the Bream, a fixed paternoster rig with a lightweight open ended or plastic mesh feeder is the obvious choice. This rig will be sensitive to hopefully produce positive bites and allow you to twitch the bait every now and then.

Hooks should be small - around 18 to 22, but hooklengths should be around 3lb. There are plenty of fish around 3 to 4lb. The rod you use is important. Traditional Bream rods have a soft through action to help prevent the hook from pulling out of the Breams' soft mouths, but they don't cast as far as a stiffer rod. Tip sensitivity is paramount.
A soft glass tip with only a slight bend is best, but look out for drop back bites as well.
A target board can be useful on those days when they're being finicky.

Types of Fish: Bream, roach, perch, and pike.

Rules/Bans:

No fires or camping allowed.
No night fishing. No live baits.
No cars or motorcycles allowed on banks. No wasp grub.
Bloodworm and joker is only allowed between Oct and March.
No litter to be left on banks.
Keep to recognised footpath.
Close all gates.

Number of Lakes: Two

Facilities:

Telephone: 07771 986849

Information kindly supplied by Doncaster & District Angling Association.

Star Carr Fishery
Brandesburton.

Ticket Price: £5.00 Day ticket, £2.00 for an extra rod.
Season tickets £70.00

Directions: Situated off the A164
Bridlington to Hull road.
Pass through Brandesburton
and just before a sharp bend
turn left to the fishery.

Description: Three lakes here at
Star Carr Fishery, two are
coarse lakes and the other is a
fly fishing pond. The larger coarse lake is three and a half
acres with 14 pegs and has a mixture species including
some large tench upto 11lb 10oz. The smaller coarse lake is
only an acre and around 9 feet deep, but is packed with
carp. Mirror, common, grass, crucian and a few rather
colourful koi, they are all in this pond. The largest carp are
upto 22lbs.

Number of Lakes: Three

Rules/Bans: No night fishing.

Facilities:

Telephone: 01964 543466   **Sat Nav:** YO25 8NB

Staddlethorpe Pond
Gilberdyke.

Ticket Price: Day tickets £5.00. OAP's, juniors £4.50. Extra rod £2.00

Direction: Leave the M62 at Junction 38 and follow the signs for Newport and Gilberdyke. When you arrive at Gilberdyke, you need to find Wards Hotel and turn left there. Then turn right onto Station Road and go over the bridge. Take a very sharp turn right and go down the unmade track to the pond.

Description: Fairly light tackle works well for most fish, but if you are setting up for the carp it may be wise to ignore the smaller fish and really beef it up. Some large carp do come out every now and again, and it is always to the anglers who target them with luncheon meat and corn. There are over 40 pegs to fish from and good depths of up to 10 ft in places. Most tactics will see you catching with caster being the late evening favourite.

Types of Fish: There are plenty of carp (including Ghosties) in the 3 to 5lb bracket but also some very big fish approaching the 30lb mark. There are also some nice tench that run up to 4lb. Bream are present and run to 5lb, with perch (3lb), orfe (4lb) and roach (1lb) making up the other stock.

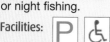 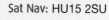

Rules/Bans: Barbless hooks only. No keepnets or night fishing.

Facilities: P   ♿   **Number of Lakes:** One

Telephone: 01405 767614   **Sat Nav:** HU15 2SU
Fishing Tackle Direct

Wansford Fishery
Wansford Trout and Coarse Fishery, Driffield.

Ticket Price: Day Ticket £4.00, extra rod £1. Under 16s £3.00

Directions: From Driffield, take the B1249 towards Skipsea. Go straight through Wansford and you will come to a sharp left hand bend, just round there you will see the signs for the fishery.

Description: This fishery caters for both trout and coarse anglers. The coarse lake has 28 pegs and is in the shape of a horse shoe. The banking is quite steep, but the pegs that are cut in, are a good size. The deepest area is nearest the trout lake, at around 7 feet. Most of the rest of the lake is an average of 5 feet. There are now plenty of matured reeds and rushes to target the carp in the margins. This is an excellent all year round fishery for both novices and more experienced angler.

Types of Fish: Carp, tench, bream, perch and roach.

Rules/Bans: No carp in keepnets, Barbless hooks, all nets to be dipped. No boilies. Groundbait in moderation.

Number of Lakes: One coarse. One trout

Facilities: P ♿ 🚻   **Sat Nav:** YO25 9HR

Telephone: 01377 240329

47

Westfield Park
Fitling.

Ticket Price: Day Tickets £5.00 on the bank.
Registered Disabled and Under 14's £3.00

Directions: Take the B1242 from Hornsea heading south.
Pass through Aldbrough and carry on towards Garton.
Once at Garton you need to take a right turn following the
tourist signs for the park. Turn left at the sign post for
Fitling. Lakes and parking are on your left hand side.

Description: This is an ideal venue for families to come and
stay a while. There are three lakes which are stocked along
similar lines. The smallest is Lake 3, this is about an acre in
size but is the deepest at 12 feet. Lake 2 is just over two
acres and has depths between 4 and 6 feet. The final lake
is the biggest at two and a half acres. Most of the lakes are
flanked by holiday cottages which are well equipped and
clean. There are some very good bream approaching
double figures, sizeable tench that average a little over 5lb
and some huge carp that almost reach 30lbs.

Types of Fish: Roach, perch, bream, carp, plus few barbel
and chub

34

Facilities: P ♿ 🍔 🚻 Accommodation available

Rules/Bans: No boilies, barbless hooks only and no keepnets
except matches.

Telephone: 01964 527353   **Sat Nav:** HU12 9AL

Westlands Lakes
Hornsea Rd, Sigglethorne, Hull.

Ticket Price: Day tickets £5.00 per rod, per day.

Directions: From Hull, travel north on the A165. When you reach White Cross turn right onto the A1035. After a couple of miles turn right onto the B1244 sign posted Hornsea. The lakes are on your right.

Description: There are six lakes at Westlands and its very hard to chose between them, they all seem to fish well. Here are the depths and species you chose! Middle Pond (34 Pegs) Depths 5-10ft. Carp to 42lbs, bream, silver fish Tench Lake (26 Pegs) Depths 6-12ft. Tench & bream to 9lbs+, chub, rudd/roach. Little Tench (25 Pegs) Depths 5-6ft. Carp, tench, ide, rudd, roach, chub, barbel. Canal Pond (32 pegs) Depth 4-5ft. Carp, ide, tench, bream, rudd, roach. Island Lake (20 pegs) Depth 3-6ft. New lake 6-12ft.

Rules/Bans: Carp anglers by appointment only. No Night fishing. Barbless Hooks Only. No trout or high oil pellets. Groundbait by pole cup and feeder only. No Fixed Leads or feeders. No Artificial Baits. No Keepnets unless in matches. All nets to be dipped and rinsed. No carp over 10lbs in nets. No cat or dog meat allowed. No tin cans allowed on the fishery (e.g. meat and sweetcorn)

Number of Lakes: Six   **Telephone:** 01964 541192   35

Facilities: **Sat Nav:** HU11 5QL
Tackle shop on site

Arial View of Westalnds Lakes   Shop

West Cowick Pond
Finnleys Lane, West Cowick.

Ticket Price: Day tickets £5.00. Extra rod £2.00. Concessions £4.50.

Directions: Leave the M62 at junction 35 and take the A1041 towards Rawcliffe, carry on towards Snaith and look for the signs for the Council Highways Department. The water is situated on the left, down a road called Finnleys Lane.

Description: Fishing is allowed from three sides of this water, which drops down to 17ft near the centre.The water is a 6-acre clay pit that offers some classic big water fishing with the benefits of being very well stocked. Bream are plentiful around all 25 well spaced pegs. There are few rarely caught large carp to 25lb weight.

Types of Fish: West Cowick Pond is a "mixed coarse fishery" with good stocks of tench, bream, rudd, roach, crucian and carp.

Rules/Bans: Barbless hooks only. No keepnets or night fishing.

Facilities: **Number of Lakes:** One

Telephone: 01405 767614   **Sat Nav:** DN14 9ED
Fishing Tackle Direct

Wholsea Grange Fishery
Skiff Lane, Holme-on-Spalding Moor.

Ticket Price: £5 for up to 2 rods. £3 for under 12's. Payable on the bank. Match bookings taken.

Directions: Turn off the A614 (Market Weighton to Howden Road) in Holme-on-Spalding Moor. After 200 yards bear right onto Skiff Lane. Drive on for 2.5 miles past the industrial estate to the end of Skiff Lane and turn left at the 'No Through' road sign. Drive for a half mile over the small bridge and to the end of the road.

Description: Another fishery with four good ponds to chose from. Pond 1 is approximately 1.5 acres, with 23 pegs. Stocked with carp to 10lb plus, roach, bream and skimmers, tench and gudgeon. The water runs to 10ft deep. The New Lake is approximately 2 acres and well stocked with small carp, ide, tench and roach. Designed as a match lake, there are 35 pegs. This water has islands, lily pads and reed beds to target with depths to approx 7ft. The Corner Pond is small and secluded with only 6 pegs. A favourite with many pleasure anglers, stocked with carp and roach. The Old Pond is a quiet and attractive small pond with 7 pegs. Recently restocked with small carp, skimmers, roach, rudd and tench. Snake Lake to open in August 09. It will be stocked with carp, skimmers, ide, tench and chub - 26 pegs.

Rules/Bans: Fishing from dawn till dusk only. No keep nets other than in matches and The Old Pond. Barbless hooks only - No braid to hook lines. No trout pellets. All under 16's must be accompanied by a adult. No pets. No litter.

Number of Lakes: Four

Telephone: 01430 860231
www.wholseafishery.co.uk
Sat Nav: YO43 4BE

Facilities: P 🚻

37

Willitoft Fishery
Spaldington.

Ticket Price: Day tickets £5.00. One rod only.

Directions: Come off the M62 motorway at Junction 37 and take the A614 towards Holme on Spalding Moor. Turn left after about 4 miles, signposted Spaldington. Take your very next right and keep on this road and the water is on the right.

Description: The two ponds cover about 3 acres in total, with the average depths between 5 and 6 ft. In total there are 45 pegs on the lakes with the majority being suitable for the angler with disabilities. Low Lake and High Lake are both similar and stocked with bream just over 2lb and good sized roach and ide. Carp reach 15lbs and if your lucky you may catch the odd chub and tench. Fishing light is your best option with bread punch or white maggot. Meat or sweetcorn for the carp.

Types of Fish: Tench, carp, ide, roach, bream, and a few chub.

Rules/Bans: Barbless hooks only and keepnets in matches only. Open from 8am till times displayed.

Facilities: P ♿ 🚻

Number of Lakes: Two

Telephone: 01757 288609   **Sat Nav:** DN14 7NP

38

Windmill Pond
New Holland.

Ticket Price: Membership permits and prices on page 60

Directions: From Barrow on Humber follow the B1206 to New Holland. Proceed though the village until you reach the cross roads. Continue straight on and follow the road/public footpath until you reach Windmill Pond. Please note that the first pond you come to is private.

Description: Windmill Pond is a mature clay pit of about three acres, situated on the South Bank of the River Humber. Yes I know it isn't in East Yorkshire but well worth crossing the bridge for. In recent years there have seen some excellent catches of rudd and perch. No fancy tactics needed here, just pole-fished maggots, bread or sweetcorn. The large number of carp that were introduced have done well and now average well over 10lb, with several fish in excess of 20lb having been reported. It could be described as an easy carp water as several fish may be caught in a session without too much difficulty. They respond well to all baits and can be caught on luncheon meat and sweetcorn, as well as boilies. It offers excellent sport for the pleasure angler in peaceful surroundings.

Facilities: P   ♿   **Number of Lakes:** One

Rules/Bans: Full list of rules can be found on page 59

Telephone: 07976 779983

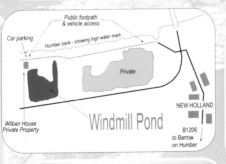

Information kindly supplied by
Hull and District Anglers'
Association.

Woodall's Pond
Newport.

Ticket Price: Day tickets £3.00. Extra rod £1.00.
Under 16's must be accompanied by an adult.

Directions: Leave the M62 at junction 38, take the B1230
heading towards Newport. When you get to the Market
Weighton Canal, turn right into Canal East Side. The pond a
short distance along on your right hand side.

Description: This is a very attractive mature two acre lake,
which offers many bankside features to target the big fish
lurking in the reeds. There are 30 pegs to choose from, with
depths of four feet at the bank to around fifteen feet in the
centre. Take a good selection of baits which should include
maggot, corn, worm, paste or soft hookable pellets.

Types of Fish: There is a good head of bream and tench in
the water. Also present are specimen carp to 30lb, pike to
20lb, chub, roach, perch, ide and eels.

Rules/Bans: No keepnets. Barbless hooks only. No peas,
nuts or beans. Ground bait in moderation.

Facilities: P 🚻 ♿   **Number of Lakes:** One

Telephone: 01430 441127   **Sat Nav:** HU15 2RL   40

Rose Cottage Pond
Landings Lane, Sandholme Landings, Newport.

Ticket Price: Day ticket £4.00 by prior arrangement.

Directions: See Map. Leave the M62 at junction 38. Take the B1230 to Newport. Turn Right onto Thimble Hall Lane, at T-Junction turn Right. The pond is on the left.

Description: An unspoilt natural pond, each peg having individual features. Well stocked with healthy good-sized fish. An enclosed, gravelled car park is available on site for fishermen. The pond itself is 2.5 acres and is an exceptionally picturesque pond with many beautiful plants and trees surrounding it. Last season the largest fish caught and weighed were: Carp 36.7lb, Bream 14.5lb, Tench 9.5lb with coarse fish bags well over 100lb easily achievable.

Types of Fish: The pond contains bream, tench, roach, rudd, perch, carp and hybrids.

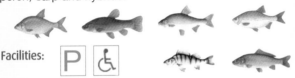

Facilities: P ♿

Number of Lakes: One

Sat Nav: HU15 2RU

Rules/Bans: Enquire before you start fishing

41

Telephone: 01430 472166 **Mob:** 0770 2645595

F I S H I N G   T E R M S

Here is a list of the words most commonly used. This will help anglers new to the sport to understand fishing terms used by other anglers.

Bale arm: A revolving arm on a fixed spool reel which winds line onto the spool.

Bagging up: A term used when an angler is catching really well, or to describe a venue that is fishing well.

Bait Bands: These are small rubber bands. They are aimed at securing difficult to hook baits to the hook. They come in various sizes to accommodate the size of the bait.

Baiting Needle: These pull the hair loop through the bait. They have a mechanism for attaching to the loop whether it is like a small hook, or a pivot that hooks over the loop. The needle is then drawn back through the bait taking the loop and hair with it.

Barbless: A type of hook without sharp barbs to help retain bait and fish. Barbed hooks are banned from most fisheries.

Bin Lids: A slang term for large bream.

Bite alarms: These are electronic sensors that detect the movement of line caused by the fish. They usually have an audible alarm or light to alert the angler.

Bivies: These are domed tents with an opening at the front providing a shelter from the elements.

Boilies: These are generally hard balls of bait that are primarily designed as a carp bait.

Bread punch: A bread punch has a circular 'punch' at the end which is pushed down onto a slice of bread and cuts a small piece out which is placed on the hook. There are many different sizes of punches for different hook sizes.

Breaking strain: The amount of pressure a line will take before snapping.

Bumped off: This term is used by pole anglers, whereby through the use of heavy tactics the fish once hooked is bumped off. This happens when the fish is not big enough to expand the elastic fully.

Casters: The chrysalis form of a maggot.

Deadbaiting: The use of dead fish for catching predatory fish such pike, perch, and eels.

Disgorger: A long device to help remove the hook from a fish's mouth. Always have one with you.

Foul Hooked: A fish that has been hooked anywhere else on the body apart from the mouth.

Groundbait: A dry mixture intended to be thrown into the water to attract fish. Usually consists of bread crumb, crushed biscuit, crushed hemp or other ingredients.

Hair Rig: A hair rig is generally a piece of line that extends beyond the point of the shank of the hook. On the end of the length of line is a small loop.

Hooklength: A short length of line, of lesser breaking strength than the mainline, to which the hook is tied. It is used to make it less likely to be detected by the fish. It also ensures that if the line is snapped by a fish, the angler would not then lose the float / swim feeder / leger and all the other shot

Legering: Bait held on the bottom by means of a weight or feeder.

Loosefeed: Small offerings of loose bait, such as maggots or sweetcorn, which are thrown into the water to keep the fish interested in the area you are fishing.

Line Bites: False indications of bites usually caused by fish brushing against the line.

Lures: Artificial fish, used to tempt predators such as pike and zander.

Margin: This is an area nearest the bank, that has a shallower depth than that of the main water.

Match fishing: A competitive form of coarse fishing which involves people drawing out a random peg (a place to fish), and then trying to catch as many fish as possible within the allotted time. Usually the winner will be the one with the greatest weight of fish caught.

Peg: A peg is a pre defined fishing area. Venues are split up into evenly spaced fishing zones which are often marked with a wooden peg or marker.

Pinkies: The larvae of the green bottle fly. Small, very lively and great as a loosefeed on stillwaters and canals or as a hookbait for smaller fish.

Plummet: A device used for determining the depth of the water in which you are fishing.

Pole: A pole is constructed from very advanced carbon combinations and comes in various sizes, weight and prices.

Pole Rig: These are lengths of line that have the float, weights and a hook attached.

Quiver tip: A special type of rod used to detect bites when ledgering. It has a sensitive tip that curves over when the angler has a bite. Quiver tips vary in strength and stiffness which can be changed according to the weather conditions.

Snags: Features in your swim that are likely to cause you problems They can also be fish holding features such as lilies, overhanging trees, sunken branches. A place to avoid once a fish is hooked.

Spade end hooks: Spade end hooks have an up-turned flattened piece of metal instead of an eye to which to tie the fishing line.

Specimen: A term given to any fish that is a particularly good size for its species.

Strike: To respond to the taking of the bait by pulling the rod in an upwards or sideways motion to hook the fish.

Swim: The area of water where you are fishing.

Tackle: A term used to refer to any fishing equipment (photo tackle)

Test curve: The test curve is the time and weight needed to make the tip bend 90 degrees from the rod butt. Each rod has a test curve with those being used for specimen fish such as carp having a greater test curve than a general coarse rod.

Trotting: Allowing a float to travel at the speed of the current.

POLE FISHING
FOR THE BEGINNER

Of all the different methods of fishing I've tried, I haven't found any of them as accurate or as easy as pole fishing. To be able to place your bait and feed to the exact spot, sometimes only inches from an island or group of reeds is what makes pole fishing so productive and fun.

TACKLE NEEDED

A Pole
Poles come in various sizes, from 4 metres (usually called a whip) to poles of 18.5 metres. They also vary dramatically in price as well, this is usually governed by weight and rigidity. The lighter and straighter (no droop at the end) the more expensive they are. I recommend a pole between 11 and 13 metres, stay away from the smaller telescopic ones. Many tackle shops have poles ready assembled for you to handle, make sure you are comfortable with its weight and it feels well balanced. Test that it takes apart smoothly. If possible, get a pole with a spare top section as they enable you to rig up for different species and size of fish.

Pole Rigs
Experienced anglers can make up their own pole rigs but beginners are advised to buy ready-made. There are plenty of quality ready made rigs available for as little as £2.99. These rigs come with a main line with a loop on the end (used to attach the line to the stonfo connector at the tip of your pole). A float with enough shot below it to cock it nicely in the water and a length of lower breaking strain line, which has a spade end hook tied to it. The float and shot can slide down the line and be adjusted accordingly.

Pole Elastic
The elastic that runs through the top sections of your pole cushions the fight of a hooked fish and allows you to play it. Elastics are graded in sizes 1-20.
The following list is a good guide for the beginner:
1. For small roach and perch for example - use a No4 elastic with a 1lb hook length and a 2lb main line.
2. If fishing for small carp and tench or skimmer bream use a No8 or 10 elastic with a 3.5lb main line and 2.5lb hook length.
3. When fishing for carp up to 12lbs use a No16 to 18 elastic, and a main line of 8lb with a 6.5lb hook length.

START TO FISH

Fishing Position
Get your seatbox in position. Ideally, when sitting on the box, your thighs should be in a horizontal position, at right angles to your lower leg. Holding the pole correctly makes it comfortable for long periods and prevents backache. For a right handed person you need to rest the pole across your knees with your left hand supporting it. Put your right forearm along the end of the pole and firmly grip the pole with your right hand. Have close to hand - your bait, landing net, disgorger and anything else you may require for your days fishing. It is important to have your pole roller in the correct location. The pole has to be well balanced in your hands when it leaves the roller - this prevents rig tangles when shipping out.

Start Fishing
You have set up your pole and plumbed your depth - so now you are ready to fish. Make sure you have between 10" and 20" of line between the tip and float. In more windy conditions you may want to lengthen this. Feed your swim with groundbait (if allowed) plus a few bits of your hook bait. This is more accurately done using a pole cup which can be fixed to the end of your pole. Put your bait on the hook and ship out your pole trying to keep your rig in the water as this prevents tangles. Lay the rig on the water lengthways. The shot on the line will pull the line under the water and cock the float.
Enjoy your first pole fishing day!

Hull & District Anglers' Association Rules

Fishery Rules:

1. No fish to be killed - all fish (including pike) must be returned. Removing or deliberately killing fish is a criminal act under the Theft Act. The Association reports all such offenses to the Police and if necessary to guarantee such cases are brought before the court will instigate a private prosecution.

2. No fish to be transferred to or from other waters. It is an offense under the Salmon & Freshwater Fisheries Act to introduce fish without the necessary permission.

3. No litter of any description, including discarded tackle, is to be left. Any angler caught deliberately leaving litter will face an immediate life ban.

4. No angler may fish more than three rods at any one time on any Association fishery.

5. No dogs or guns of any description to be brought on to Association fisheries.

6. No gaffs or pike gags are allowed on Association fisheries.

7. No angler is permitted on any Association fishery between the hours of 10pm and 5am (Carlton on Trent is 10pm to 7am), except where the member is in possession of a Night Fishing Permit. Members (other than Association bailiffs) who do not possess a night permit and are found on any Association fishery during the hours stated (whether they are actually fishing or not) shall be liable to have their membership permit revoked and shall face possible prosecution for trespass.

8. Tackle must not be left in the water unattended.

9. No fires, swimming or boating.

10. Follow the Country Code. Keep gates closed. Park in such a manner that problems are not caused to other anglers, landowners, farmers or members of the public. The Officers reserve the right to sanction the towing away, or clamping, of vehicles parked in an irresponsible manner. The Officers disclaim any liability for damage caused by such action and membership signifies acceptance of these conditions.

11. Behave responsibly and respect other anglers using fisheries. Do not damage trees or bushes and do not interfere with the wildlife.

12. Children under 14 years of age must be accompanied by an adult.

13. The use of keepsacks (carp sacks) and/or retaining tubes is not allowed on any Association Fishery.

14. Any person found to be negotiating for waters held by the Association shall forfeit the right of membership for life.

15. Fused braid is not to be used as a hookline, nor should it be used as a main line without a leader of nylon at least the length of the rod.

16. No keepnets to be used on Motorway Pond, Tilery Lake or the Brough Complex (unless authorised by the Association's committee).

17. Anyone fishing deliberately for pike or carp must be in possession of a landing net with arms not less than 36 inches in length. The net must be of soft knotless material.

18. The following applies to anglers who are specifically fishing for pike. Wire traces must always be used and must not be less than 15 inches in length. In addition, when fishing live baits or dead baits, treble hooks larger than size 8 must not be used and must not be made of stainless steel and treble hooks must not be used that have more than one barb per hook. Traces and main line must not be less than 12lb breaking strain.

19. On the Tilery and Brickyard venues, no angler shall manoeuvre a bait-boat, with the purposes of dropping baited hooks or free offerings, at a greater range than he/she can cast. Any member suspected of fishing at excessive range, can be asked by any Bailiff or Night Permit Holder, to prove by casting the distance he/she is fishing. Failure to either cast the distance or a refusal to cast will be reported to the next Delegates Meeting.

20. When deliberately fishing for carp on any Association water the minimum breaking strength of line for marker float set-ups, spodding or fishing will be 12lb breaking strain.

21. The use of unhooking mats is allowed and encouraged on all Association Fisheries

22. The use of weight slings is allowed on all Association Fisheries.

23. Fishing is only allowed from designated swims.

24. Night Permit waiting lists will be published on the Associations website.

25. Barbless hooks must be used at all times on Hawk Pond at the Brough Complex.

Hull & District Anglers' Association Membership Costs

Hull and District Anglers' Association
1st January until 31st December

Adult £34 plus £17 joining fee
Senior (over 65) £17 plus £8 joining fee
Junior (under 17) £11 no joining fee

Membership Permits are available from the following shops:

The Compleat Angler
58 Chanterlands Avenue
Hull
HU5 3TT
Tel: 01482 346842

The Fishing Shop
293 Ings Road
Hull
HU8 0NB
Tel: 01482 781926

Fishing Basket
470 Beverley Road
Hull
HU5 1NE
Tel: 01482 445284

Newport News Agency
Main Street
Newport
01430 440308

Beverley Angling Centre
8 Maple Drive
Beverley
HU17 9QJ
Tel: 01482 869948

Discount Fishing Tackle
648 Anlaby Road
Hull
HU3 6UU
Tel: 01482 500105

Everetts Angling and Outdoor World
Holderness Road
Hull
Tel: 01482 374201

The Fishing Shop
293 Ings Road
Hull
HU8 0NB
Tel: 01482 781926

Permits may also be obtained by post from:
HDAA
PO Box 188
Hull
HU9 1AN

Bradford No1 Angling Association Membership Costs

Subscriptions:

Juniors	(under 17 years old)	£14
Ladies		£16
Veteran	(over 65 years old)	£16
Full "Senior (male)"	(over 17 years old)	£36
Joining Fee	(not Juniors)	£20
Second rod permit	(allows 2nd rod on all venues)	£14
Privilege tickets	(allows a guest with full adult)	£3
Night Fishing	(Allows night fishing on either Knoford or Kirkless lagoons)	£50

East Riding of Yorkshire Tackle Shops

A & D Angling, 50 Newbridge Road, Hull.   01482 227171

A & D Angling Hedon, 1c George St, Hedon, Hull.   01482 891479

Angler's Corner Tackle Shop, 831 Hessle High Road, Hull.   01482 507350

Beverley Angling Centre, 8 Maple Drive, Beverley.   01482 869948

Blue Sky Angling Ltd, Emmotland, Driffield.   01262 481271

Complete Angler, 58 Chanterlands Avenue, Hull.   01482 346842

Discount Fishing Tackle, 648 Anlaby Road, Hull.   01482 500105

East Coast Tackle, 1b Willows Drive, Hornsea,   01964 535064

Everetts Fishing Tackle, 691 Holderness Road, Hull.   01482 374201

Fishing Basket, 500 Beverley Road, Hull.   01482 445284

The Fishing Shop, 293 Ings Rd, Hull.   01482 781926

The Tackle Shop, 969 Spring Bank West, Hull   01482 562754

Fishing Tackle Direct, 25 Westfield Avenue, Goole.   01405 767614

Fishing Republic, Southcoates Lane, Hull.   01482 707977

Harry's of Bridlington, 12 Hilderthorpe Rd, Bridlington.   01262 678045

Hedon Angling Centre, 1c George Street, Hedon, Nr Hull.   01482 891479

Matchman (Hull), 794 Beverly High Road, Hull.   01482 853193

North Bay Angling, 84 Promenade, Bridlington.   01262 401144

R.S Tackle & Guns, Unit 1, Carlisle Street, Goole.   01405 720292

Top Sports, 118 Queen Street, Withernsea.   01964 612340

Tri-Star Angling, The Boat Yard, Chapel Lane, Driffield.   01262 468688

Westlands, Hornsea Rd, Sigglesthorne, Hull.   01964 541192

Worms UK, The Mallard, Hull Rd, Seaton, Hull.   01964 532660

I N D E X

East Riding of Yorkshire

Aire & Calder Canal   12
Barmston Farm Fishing Lake   13
Beverley Canal   14
Blue Lagoon Pond   15
Brandesburton Ponds No 2   16
Brandesburton Ponds No 3+4   17
Brickyard Pond   18
Burshill A Pond   19
Burshill B Pond   20
Burton Constable   21
Driffield Canal   22
Emmotland Ponds   23
Fishponds Fishery   24
Fossehill Fisheries   25
Greaves End Pond   26
Halcyon House   27
Halsham Ponds   28
Hornsea Mere   29
Lakeminster Park Lakes   30
Lakeside   31
Lambwath Lakes   32
Market Weighton Canal   33
Moorfield Farm Fishery   34
Motorway Pond   35
Newbridge Lakes   36
Oakland Waters   37
Pastures Fish Pond   38
Rainbow Lake   39
Risby Park Fisheries   40
Rose Cottage Pond   55
Rush Lyvars Lake   41
Sandholme Lodge   42
Southfield Reservoir   43
Star Carr Fishery   44
Straddlethorpe Pond   45
Wansford Fishery   46
Westfield Park   47
Westlands Lakes   48
West Cowick Pond   49
Wholsea Grange Fishery   50
Willitoft Fishery   51
Windmill Pond   52
Woodall's Pond   53

If you know of a fishery that is not included in this guide or you want to update an existing venue. Please fill in the form below.

Fishery Name

Fishery Address

Post code

Contact Name

Telephone No

| Adult Day Ticket Price | £ | concession OAP'S | £ |

Fish species and approximate weights

Brief Description

Rules / Bans

Facilities

Number of Lakes

Please e-mail or post a colour photo for inclusion in the next publication.

Please return this form to:
Arc Publishing
166 Knowle Lane,
Bents Green,
Sheffield S11 9SJ.

chris_keeling@tiscali.co.uk

New Fishery ☐

Update to Fishery ☐

New Fishery / Fishery Update Form

NOTES